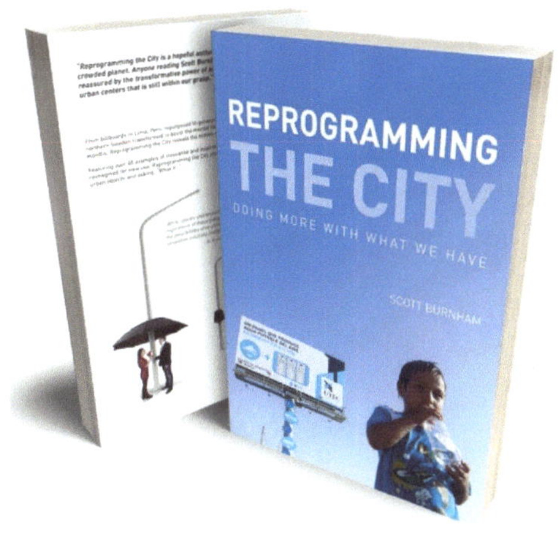

"A hopeful anthology of solutions for our hot, crowded planet. Anyone reading Scott Burnham's essential book will emerge reassured by the transformative power of creativity in the world's urban centers."

– Renée Loth, AchitectureBoston

This toolkit was created as a self-guided exercise to help people unlock the hidden potential of existing urban assets. It is even more effective when using it as a companion to the Reprogramming the City book, which contains case studies of 44 of the most innovative urban reuse projects from 17 countries.

REPROGRAMMINGTHECITY.COM/BOOK

Reprogramming the City
Toolkit Version 1.0
Print Edition
January 2020

ISBN: 978-1-945971-02-0

REPROGRAMMINGTHECITY.COM

INTRODUCTION

This toolkit is the result of a decade of work, research, and workshops I have conducted around the world as part of the Reprogramming the City initiative to help people improve cities by using existing urban assets in new ways.

The catalyst for Reprogramming the City and particularly this toolkit is to provide people with the tools to address a pressing problem: the new reality facing cities is one of limited resources. Whether financial, spatial, or material, the content of cities is finite. Yet the *context* of that content - *how* we use the assets we already have - is where the opportunity exists to respond to increasing urban needs using limited resources.

This collection of examples, insights, and exercises was assembled to help you build the tools and, most importantly, the mindset to unlock potential in existing urban assets - to do more with the structures, surfaces, and assets already in place.

This toolkit is meant to serve as a companion to the Reprogramming the City book. The book is a global overview of how the urban landscape's untapped potential is being utilized to improve life in cities using what already exists in new ways. For more information and to purchase the Reprogramming the City book, please visit **www.reprogrammingthecity.com**

Thank you for joining me on this journey to transform limited urban resources into platforms of possibility.

Scott

Scott Burnham
Founder, Reprogramming the City

BEFORE WE BEGIN...

A professor went to visit a famous Zen master. While the master quietly served tea, the professor told him everything he knew about Zen.

The master poured the visitor's cup to the brim, and then kept pouring. The professor saw the overflowing cup and exclaimed: "It's full! No more will go in!"

"This is you," the Zen master replied, pointing to the cup.

"How can I show you anything new unless you first empty your cup?"

WE ARE HERE:

THE CONTENT OF CITIES IS LIMITED.

A resilient future depends on us realizing:

ITS CONTEXT OF USE IS NOT.

Here's what that looks like...

CONTENT
This is New York's Tri-Borough Bridge. It does what bridges are supposed to do: it moves vehicles and people across the water. It is a piece of urban content.
CONTEXT
For a Red-tailed Hawk, the bridge provides shelter and support for its nest. The Hawk uses the bridge in a more beneficial context than its original function.

CONTENT
The Ammerud Underpass in Oslo does what it is supposed to do. But people who use it each day dread the dark, dirty, experience. It is content that could do more.
CONTEXT
After residents and architecture students worked together to discover its hidden potential, it is now a bright "underpass of activities" and a point of pride for residents.
TUNNELEN

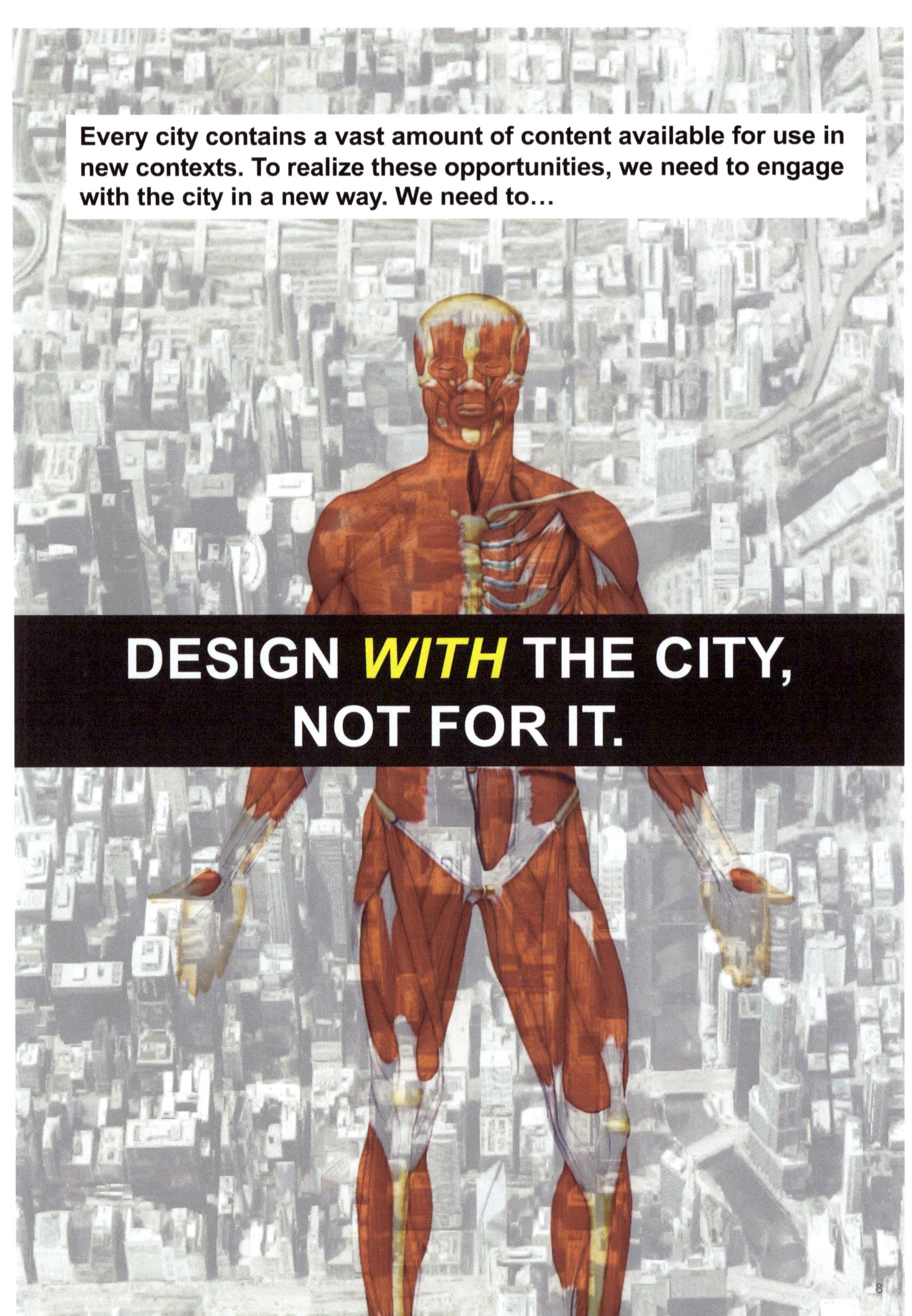
Every city contains a vast amount of content available for use in new contexts. To realize these opportunities, we need to engage with the city in a new way. We need to...
DESIGN WITH THE CITY,
NOT FOR IT.

THE POWER OF THIS COULD

Designing *with* the city transforms its limited resources into platforms of possibility.

The first step to unlock the potential of existing assets is to change our mindset from "this is" to "this could":

Most people view the world in terms of "this is": objects with fixed identities performing fixed functions. But problems aren't solved by settling for what *is*.

Solutions come from imagining what *could* be.

To understand the power of "this could," get one of these and go to the next page.

THE POWER OF THIS COULD

Harvard psychologist Ellen Langer conducted an experiment in which two groups made errors on an exercise while using a pencil. One group was given a rubber band and told:

"THIS IS
A RUBBER BAND."

In that group, **3%** realized the rubber band could also be used as an eraser.

The other group was given a rubber band and told:

"THIS COULD
BE A RUBBER BAND."

In that group, **40%** of realized it could be used as an eraser.

That's a lot of extra ability unlocked by two words.

FROM THIS IS TO THIS COULD

Moving from "this is" to "this could" transforms the potential of everything around us. For example, most look at a billboard and think "This is a source of revenue":

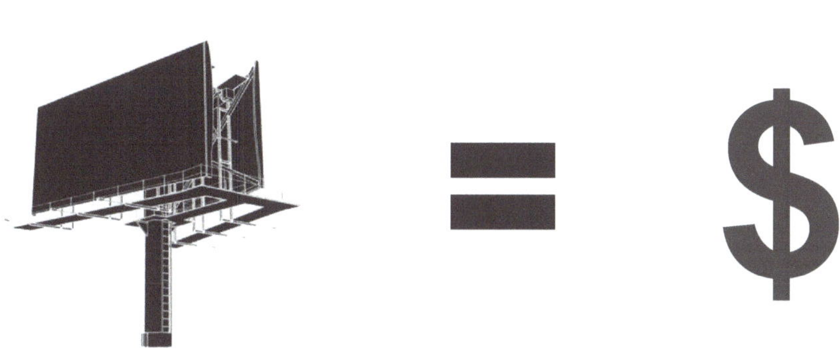

Given the amount of material, engineering, and structural capacity contained in a billboard, "this is" ignores any potential it may contain beyond its identity as a source of revenue.

What if we approached it with "this could" thinking? Instead of closing off a billboard's potential, those two words encourage an exploration of possibilities. The billboard *could* be a source of drinking water, an energy source, a device to increase the biodiversity in a city, even a structure to provide housing.

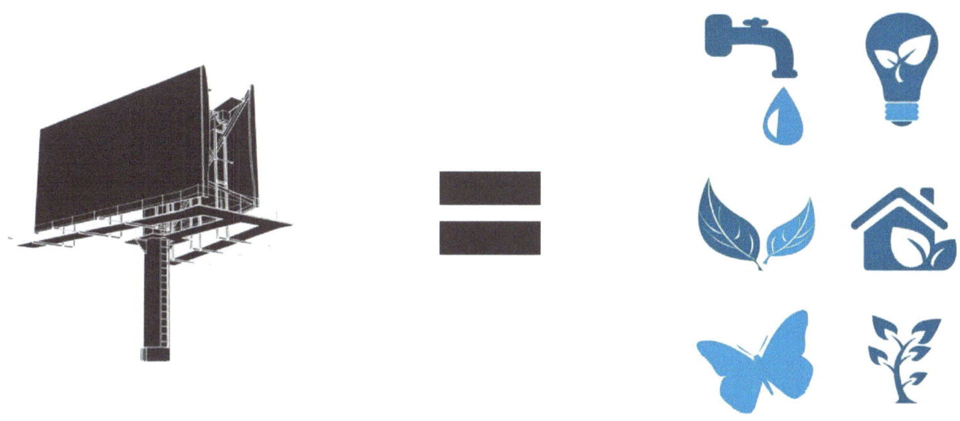

Billboards have been used for all these purposes, and more. Here's one example...

FROM THIS IS TO THIS COULD

EXAMPLE

WATER BILLBOARD

UTEC, Lima, Peru

In Lima, Peru, engineers repurposed an existing billboard to generate clean drinking water for residents in an outlying area of the city. Using reverse osmosis machines, the Water Billboard now condenses the air's humidity, then filters and cleans it of air-born impurities. At the base of the billboard, residents can simply turn on a tap to get clean drinking water.

In its first three months of operation, the billboard produced over 9,000 liters (2,380 gallons) of fresh water, fulfilling the needs of hundreds of local families who lacked access to clean drinking water.

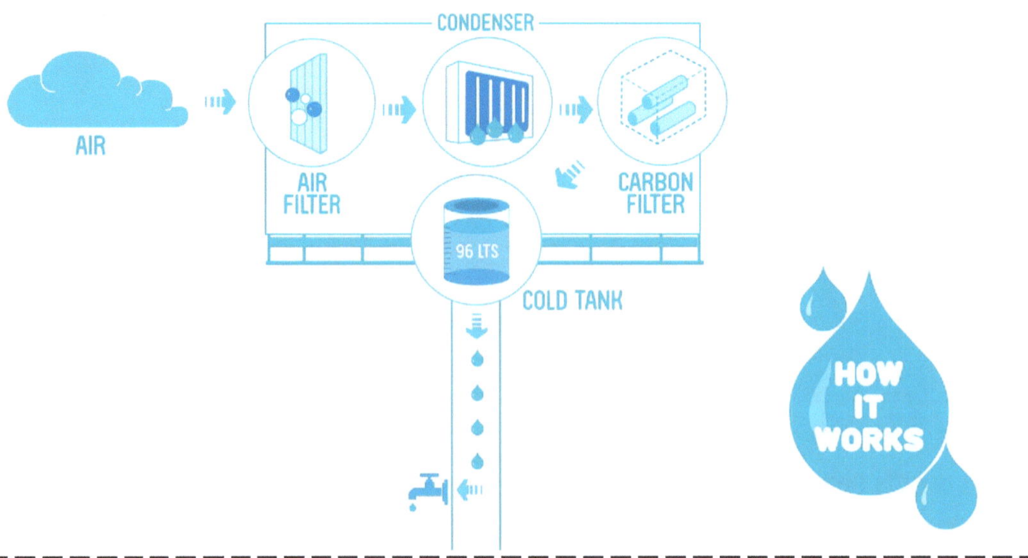

FROM THIS IS TO THIS COULD

EXAMPLE

THE CASCADE

Edge Design Institute, Hong Kong

Given the extreme density of Hong Kong, there is little room for new social infrastructure or spaces for rest and relaxation. Local firm Edge Design Institute realized that there may not be open space available, but there were plenty of stairways available for additional use.

Located next to the Centrium complex in the city's central business district, The Cascade is a mini urban park designed to fit on top of a stairway, offering people a moment of rest and relaxation. Containing green fauna, individual and group seating areas, and a lighting scheme that changes with the area's nighttime atmosphere, The Cascade transforms a single-function stairway into a multifunctional social space.

FROM THIS IS TO THIS COULD

Seeing the city's existing assets as containers of opportunity for new use transforms the limited resources of the urban landscape into platforms of possibility:

This is a billboard.

This could be a source of drinking water.

This is a stairway.

This could be a social space.

By the end of this tool kit, you will be able to fill in these squares:

This is a...

This could...

CONTAINERS OF POSSIBILITY

The most functional pieces of content have the potential to do more than their original function and make the city a better place, using what is already at hand.

"There is music in all things, if men had ears."

- Lord Byron

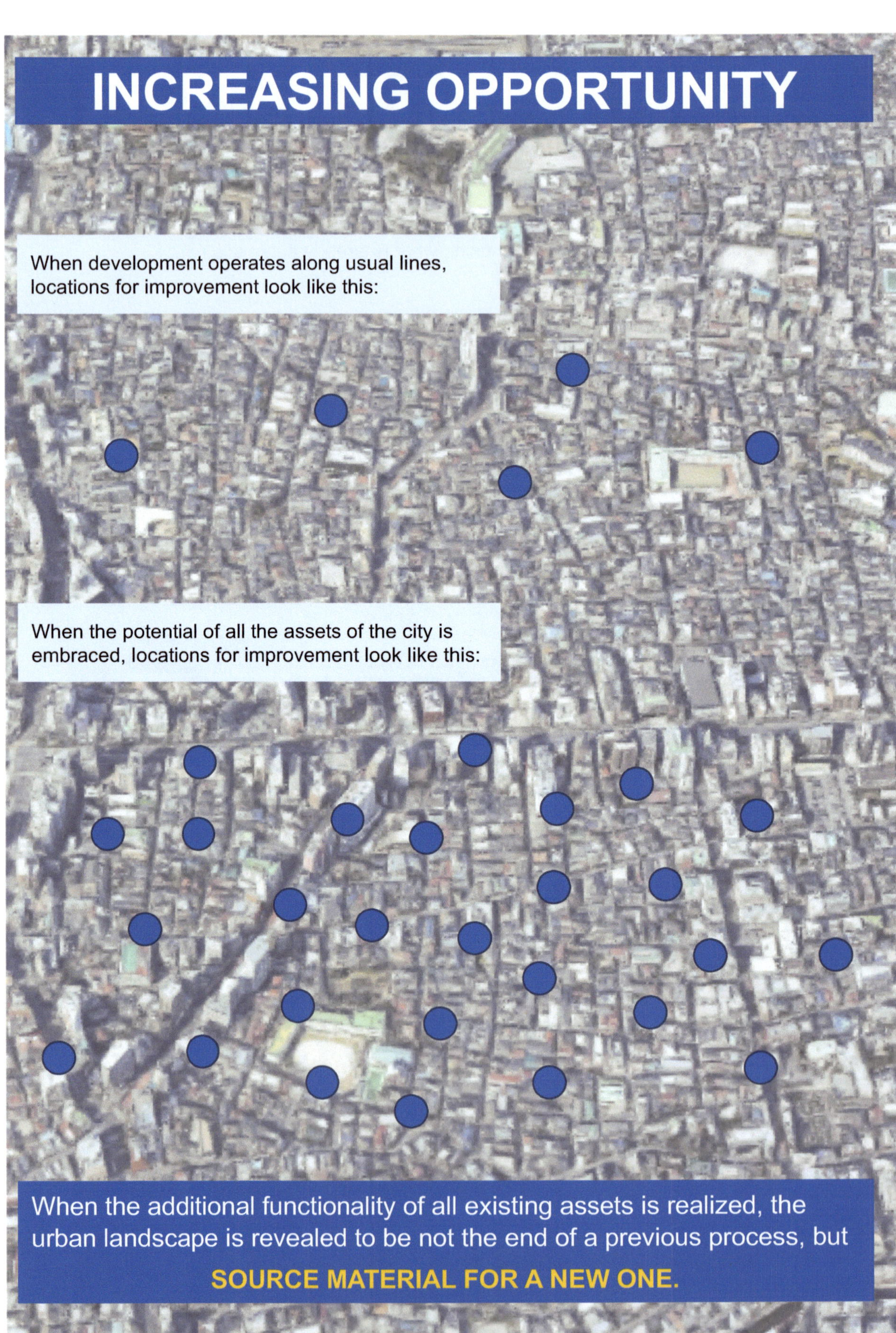
INCREASING OPPORTUNITY
When development operates along usual lines, locations for improvement look like this:
When the potential of all the assets of the city is embraced, locations for improvement look like this:
When the additional functionality of all existing assets is realized, the urban landscape is revealed to be not the end of a previous process, but
SOURCE MATERIAL FOR A NEW ONE.

NOW IT IS TIME TO REIMAGINE THE POTENTIAL OF YOUR CITY.

The following pages will help you unlock hidden potential from the city's existing assets.

UNLOCKING POTENTIAL

The process of discovering the city's untapped potential looks like this:

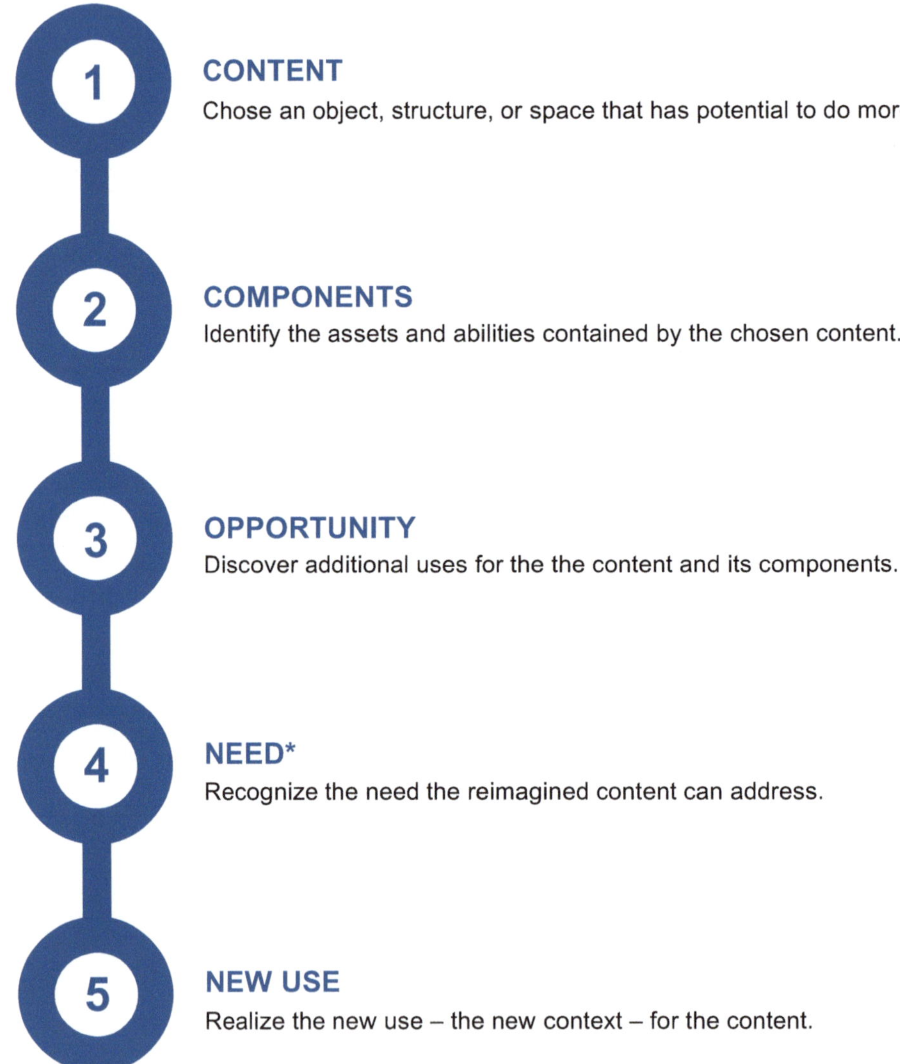

*In this process, need comes later than usual in order to build tools and capabilities first. Think of it like driving a car into an auto repair shop to be fixed – the mechanics don't know what is wrong with the car, but they know they have the tools to fix it.

1) CONTENT

1. Think of a section of your city: your neighborhood, the area you work in, etc.

2. On the grid below, sketch an aerial view of the area and note the objects, systems, and spaces—the content—the area contains. Try to list every*thing* in the area.

Content

CONTENT

List the pieces of content that caught your attention: traffic lights, subway vents, benches, bus stops, light poles, walls, fences…

Content

2) COMPONENTS

The first step in discovering the additional potential of existing urban content is to examine its components.

For example, if we examined a cup of coffee, its components would be the cup, the lid, the coffee, its lid, and so on.

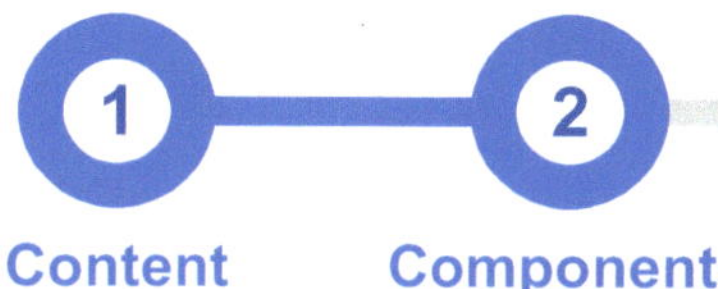

COMPONENTS

Let's look at a bus stop and its components in the same way.

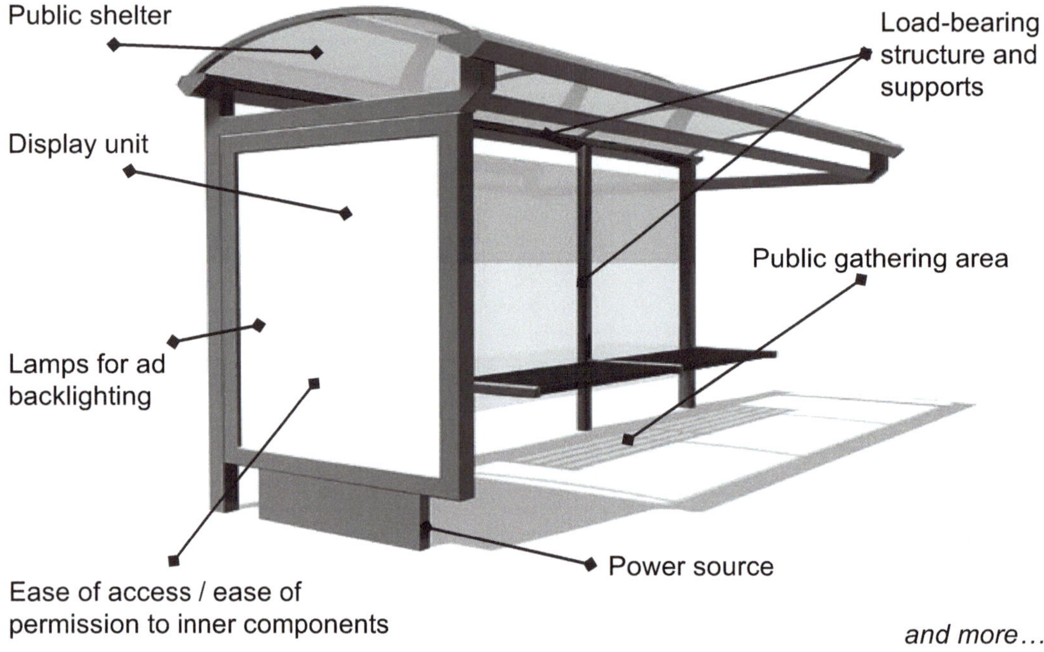

By identifying an object's components, its capacity for additional use - its *extra ability* - is also identified.

Here's how one city put the components of its bus stop to additional use…

LEVERAGING COMPONENTS

EXAMPLE

BUS STOP LIGHT THERAPY

Umeå Energi, Umeå, Sweden

Three hundred kilometers north of Stockholm, the city of Umeå, Sweden, receives almost no daylight during the winter, which impacts the mental health of its citizens. The city's energy company used the extra ability of a bus stop to counter this by replacing the bus stop's advertising bulbs with natural light frequency bulbs in 30 bus stops.

Commuters can now spend a few minutes facing the therapeutic lights while waiting for the bus to get the benefits of natural light they miss during the region's dark winter months. After the lights were installed, bus use in the city doubled.

COMPONENT ANALYSIS

Choose a piece of content you identified in your city and examine its components.

CONTENT:

WHAT IS ITS FUNCTION?

OBJECT

- ☐ Electricity
- ☐ Water
- ☐ Passage
- ☐ Connectivity (phone, data)
- ☐ Ventilation
- ☐

SPACE

- ☐ Social
- ☐ Educational
- ☐ Engagement
- ☐ Economic (skill-building)
- ☐ Wellbeing
- ☐

WHAT ARE ITS QUALITIES?

- ☐ Foundation
- ☐ Supporting structure
- ☐ Location
- ☐ Easy public access
- ☐ Shelter
- ☐ Unused or obsolete
- ☐ Historical
- ☐

OTHER ATTRIBUTES:

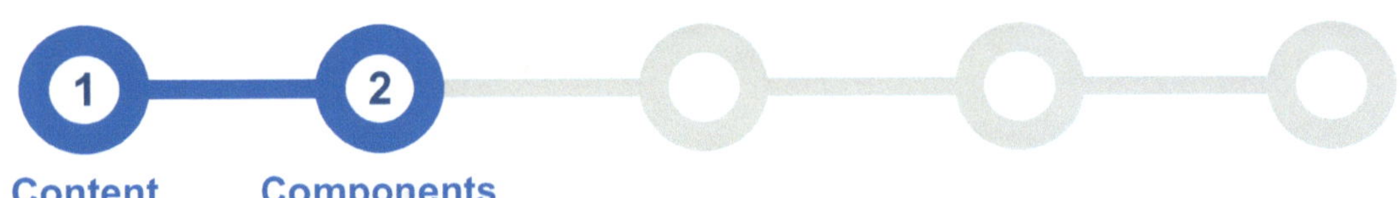

IDENTIFY COMPONENTS

Write or sketch your chosen piece of urban content and the components it contains:

CONTENT:

COMPONENTS:

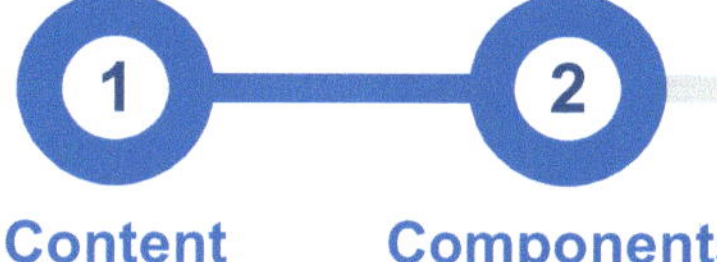

3) OPPORTUNITY

CONTENT:

COMPONENTS:

With the content's components - its extra abilities - identified, think of possible opportunities:

- ☐ Can its connectivity be extended for additional use?
- ☐ Can its function or service be improved?
- ☐ Can it host a plug-in structure or service?
- ☐ Can it be upgraded for another function?
- ☐ Can it be a platform for another activity?
- ☐ Can it be revitalized to have a second life?

What *else* could it do?

What *else* could it be?

CAPTURING OPPORTUNITY

Sometimes opportunity presents itself so clearly it should be captured right away. If you find yourself there, list your chosen content, its components, and the opportunity it presents.

Or you can continue to see how need can feed opportunity.

CONTENT:

COMPONENTS:

OPPORTUNITY:

NEW USE:

4) NEED

Now that you have a sense of the content, components, and opportunities available, think of the needs that exist in your community or city it could respond to.

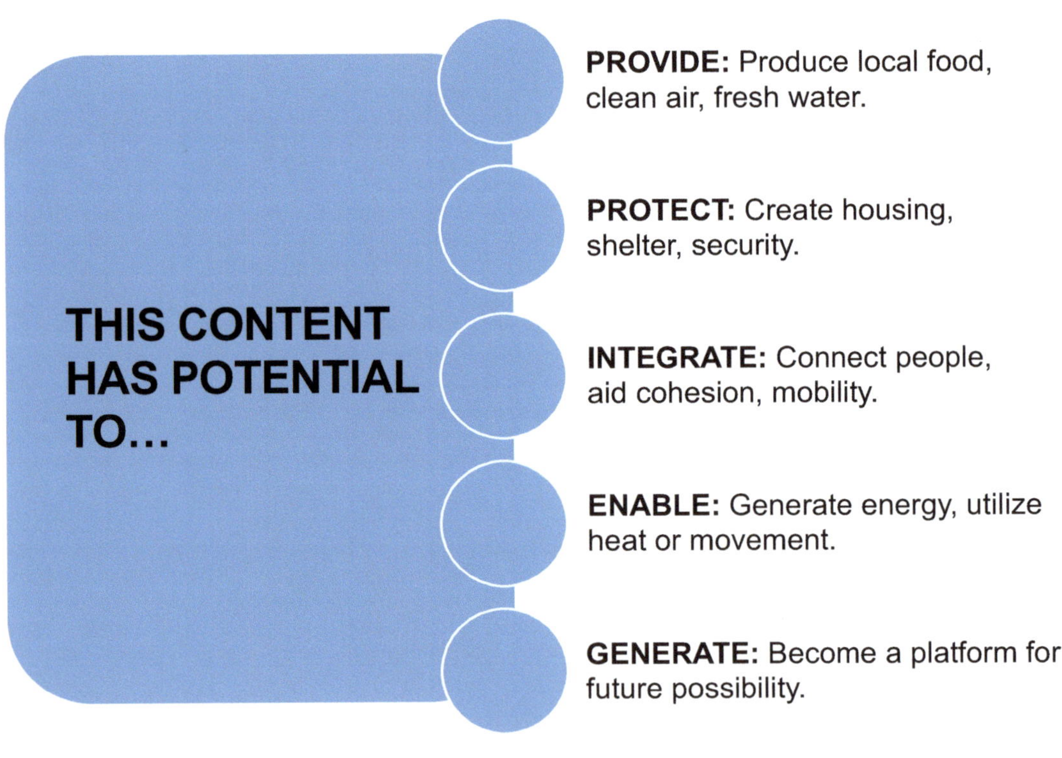

IDENTIFY THE NEED

Identify a need your chosen piece of content and its components could address:

MEETING THE NEED

EXAMPLE

BORNÉO PROJECT

Association des Designers Industriels du Québec, Montreal, Canada

Montreal wanted to reduce the amount of plastic waste in the city. "The mission," says Bornéo Project member Thomas-Eric Béliveau, "was to design an urban water source that would be a replacement for plastic water bottles."

Montreal's fire hydrants, like most in North America, are fed from the same water source as public drinking water. With a public water network already in place supplying the hydrants, the team designed an attachment that converts previously single-function hydrants into multi-functioning public water fountains.

Working with local fire officials, the Bornéo devices were designed to increase the function of hydrants without impacting their vital core purpose. They detach easily using standard fire department wrenches so firefighters can use the hydrants in emergency situations.

NEED, EXTRA ABILITY, OPPORTUNITY

This is what the need, extra ability, and opportunity in Montreal looks like:

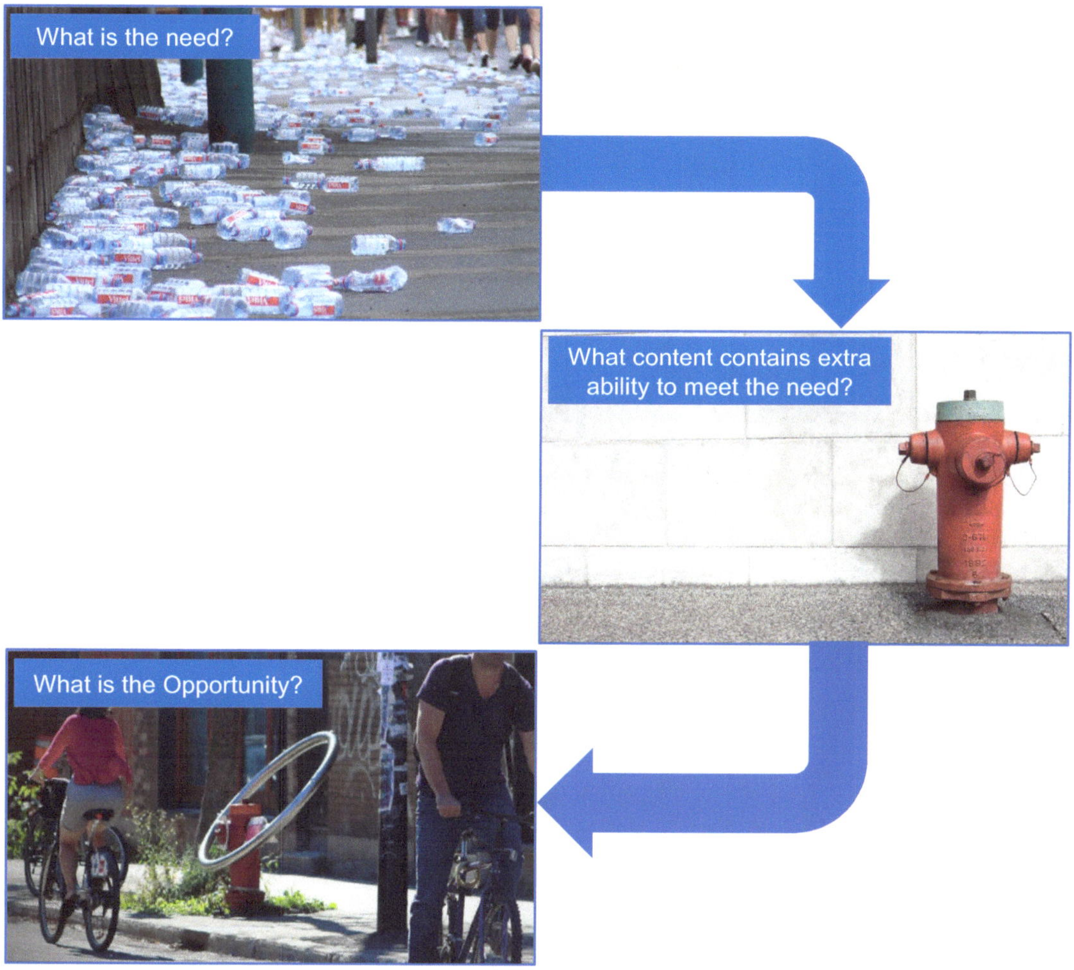

What is the need?
What content contains extra ability to meet the need?
What is the Opportunity?

1 Content — 2 Components — 3 Opportunity — 4 Need

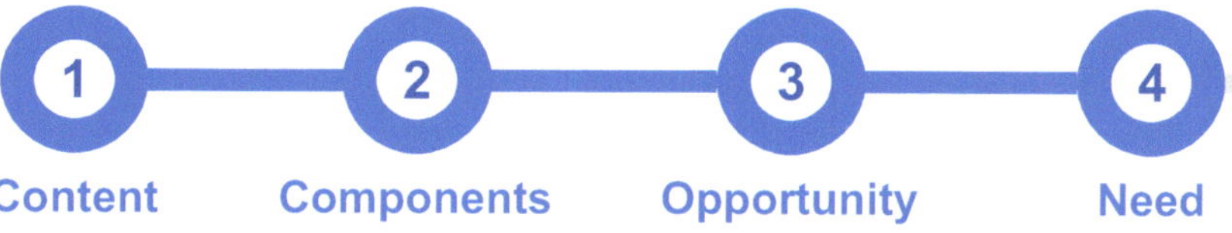

MEETING THE NEED

Use the same diagram to explore a solution for your need using the extra ability of something in the city and its opportunity to meet a need.

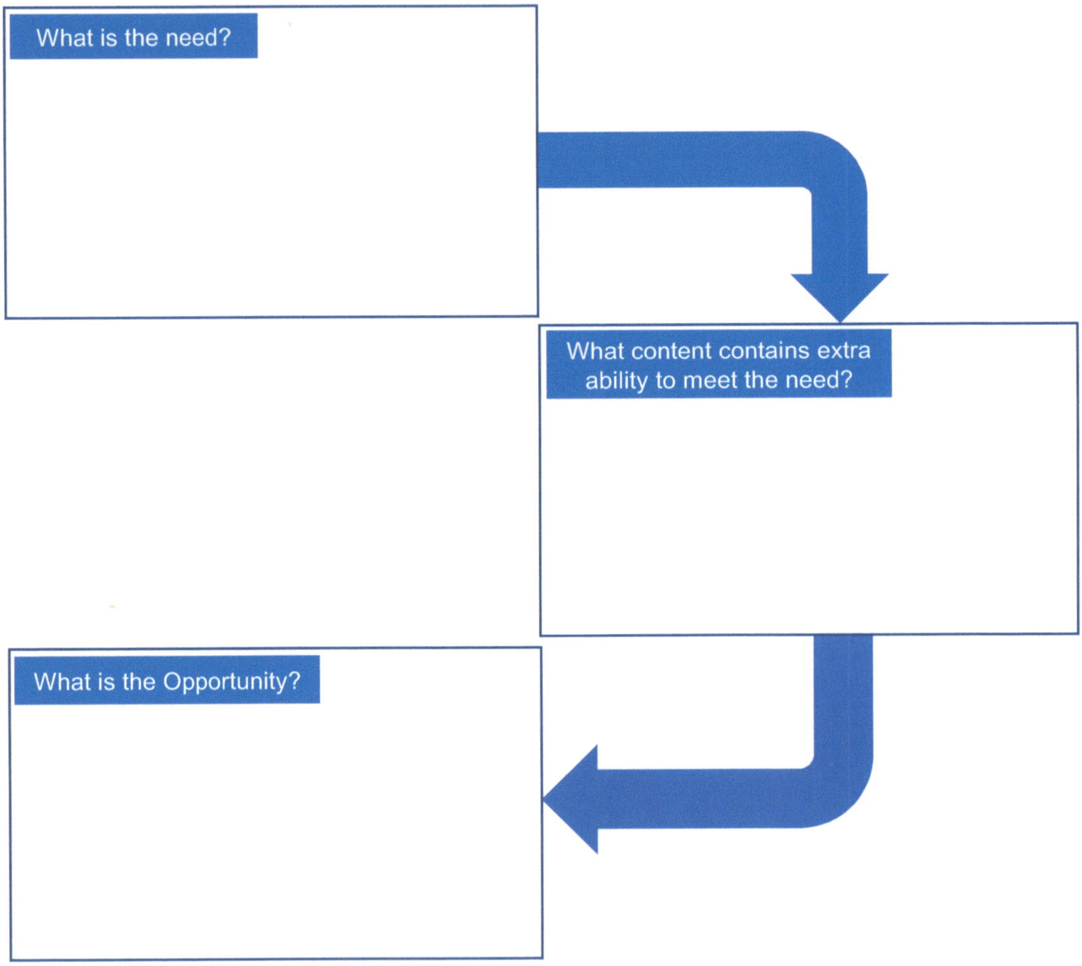

What is the need?

What content contains extra ability to meet the need?

What is the Opportunity?

5) NEW USE

What is the new use (new context) for the content?

BONUS ROUND
MAKING IT HAPPEN

THE PATH TO REALITY

It all starts with an idea.

When the *BEST. IDEA. EVER.* strikes, instinct is to make it bold and big. But cities are tough places to make new ideas happen. It is important to remember that the desire to "go big or go home" usually means:

GO BIG = GO HOME

The key is to identify the Minimal Viable Project that will bring your core idea to life.

Minimal Viable Project (MVP) is a tweaked version of the Minimal Viable Product approach taken by startup companies - stripping away all the bells and whistles beyond the product's core offering in order to get it to the marketplace quickly. The same rules apply to innovative urban projects.

Whatever the desired result is, be sure that you have a stripped-down MVP in place that captures the intent of your project. Everything can move to a version 2.0 after its launch, but don't risk the launch by betting it all on beginning big.

**"It's not the notes you play.
It's the notes you don't play."**

- Miles Davis

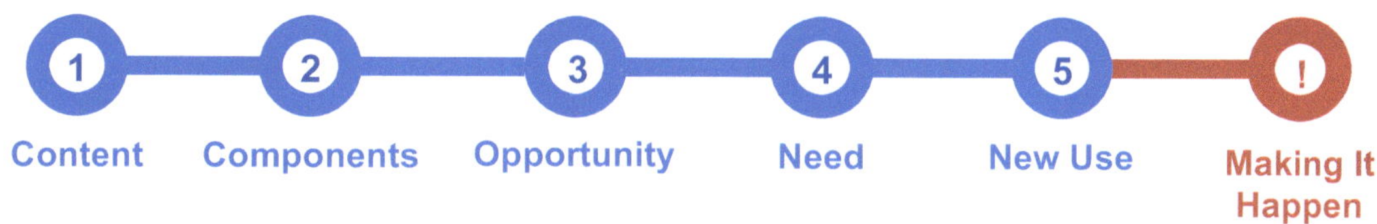

IDENTIFYING YOUR MVP

Reverse engineer your idea to find the core deliverable – the Minimal Viable Project – that will make it happen.

What is your idea for using an existing asset in a new way?

With a limitless budget, full permissions, etc., what would it look like?

Anticipating some constraints, how could it still happen?

With little money and buy-in, what is the MVP to make it happen?

1 Content · 2 Components · 3 Opportunity · 4 Need · 5 New Use · ! Making It Happen

MVP FOR THE WIN

The MVP to make my idea happen is:

To do this, I will need the help or support of:

The materials and skill sets I will need are:

The first three steps to move it forward are:

1)

2)

3)

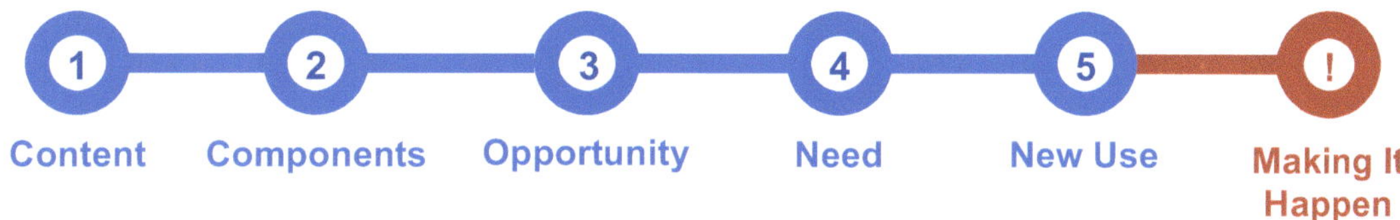

SUMMARY

Now that you have your core idea and steps towards making it happen defined, you've won. If your idea comes to life, great. If it doesn't, you're still on the path to making a big difference in the world. Really.

You've now got one of the most powerful tools anyone can posses: the ability to think in terms of "this could" instead of settling for "this is." Don't lose that ability – not that it is easy to lose once you see its power.

The next time you are faced with a challenge in your city or any part of your life, remember how "this could" changes everything after those words appear, verbally or mentally. Everything most take for granted as "this is," *could* be something else.

Most importantly, you've learned some tools that can help others. Use them. Help others discover untapped potential in the things they already have. "This could" doesn't only help you change the world - as the rubber hand experiment showed, just introducing something to others with those words expands people's minds and awareness of options.

Share the thinking and assist others to think the same way.

"You'll never catch me bragging about goals, but I'll talk all you want about my assists."

- Wayne Gretzky

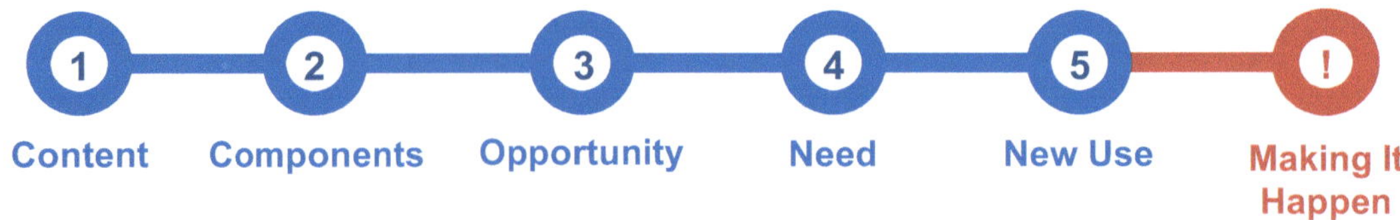

WORKSHOPS

Reprogramming the City workshops have taken place in numerous cities throughout the world. This toolkit contains the workshop's core components, but nothing can replace a guided hands-on session.

To learn more about Reprogramming the City workshops, visit: **https://reprogrammingthecity.com/workshops/**

FOR MORE INFORMATION

Scott Burnham, FRSA
sb@scottburnham.com
scottburnham.com
reprogrammingthecity.com

www.ingramcontent.com/pod-product-compliance
Lightning Source LLC
Chambersburg PA
CBHW041244040426
42445CB00005B/142
* 9 7 8 1 9 4 5 9 7 1 0 2 0 *